Evan "The Strangler" Lewis: The Most Feared Wrestler of the 19th Century

By

Ken Zimmerman Jr.

Evan "The Strangler" Lewis: The Most Feared Wrestler of the 19th Century

Copyright 2015 by Ken Zimmerman Jr. Published by Ken Zimmerman Jr. Enterprises www.kenzimmermanjr.com

All rights reserved. No portion of this book may be reproduced, stored in a retrieval system, or transmitted in any form or by any means—electronic, mechanical, photocopy, recording, or any other—except for brief quotations in printed reviews, without the prior permission of the publisher.

The work here is my own and the opinions stated are my own. The information is provided on an as-is basis. I make no representations to accuracy, completeness, suitability, validity or timeliness of any information in this book. I will not be liable for any errors, delays or omissions nor any losses, damages or injuries arising from its use.

First Edition: March 2015

If you like this book, you can sign up for Ken's newsletter to receive information about future book releases. You can sign up for the newsletter and receive bonus e-books by going to www.kenzimmermanjr.com and signing up for the monthly newsletter.

Table of Contents

Dedication 7
Introduction – The Strangler 8
Chapter 1 – "The Strangler" Arrives on the Scene 13
Chapter 2 – Acton, Marriage and More Controversy 23
Chapter 3 – Victories in the Ring and Challenges Outside It 36
Chapter 4 – A Tough New Opponent 53
Chapter 5 – Old Foes and New Challenges 65
Chapter 6 – The Quest to Be Recognized as Champion 72
Chapter 7 – Illness and End of Title Run 83
Chapter 8 – Defeat and Retirement 97
Conclusion 110
Bibliography 114
About the Author 118
Endnotes 119

Dedication

This book is dedicated to my sons, Kenneth W. Zimmerman III and Caleb M. Zimmerman. I hope combat sports continues to be a passion as they grow up.

Introduction – The Strangler

The Japanese wrestler desperately grabbed at the waist of the muscular man whose powerful right arm around his neck squeezed his neck tighter and tighter. In one last spasm before going out, Sorakichi Matsada flailed his arm before passing out. The referee was slow to respond. In a move which can kill a man, "The Strangler" continued to squeeze the now lifeless body of his opponent.

After the referee finally tapped Lewis on the shoulder, "The Strangler" smirked and dropped the lifeless Sorakichi onto the mat. Lewis nonchalantly walked away from another victim of his famous "hang hold".

The most feared professional wrestler of the 19th Century never won the World Heavyweight Championship although he held the American Championship for several years. He wasn't the biggest wrestler either. Evan "Strangler" Lewis stood 5'09" tall and weighed between 170 and 208 pounds. Normally, he weighed about 180 pounds for his matches.

Yet between 1882 and 1899, most professional wrestlers in the United States avoided "The Strangler". Many times they would only wrestle Lewis if his stranglehold was banned. City officials also sometimes demanded the stranglehold be banned to allow his matches to take place.

Wrestlers avoided Evan Lewis for two reasons. Lewis possessed above average submission skills including perfecting his stranglehold. He also possessed a pronounced mean streak. Lewis often injured wrestlers on purpose if they angered him. His two matches with Sorakichi Matsada forever cast him as the villain in the eyes of the wrestling public. Lewis' indifference to this disdain only made it worse. Other wrestlers were forgiven for things Lewis never would be.

Oddly, Lewis also often took part in prearranged matches including a couple with "Little Demon" Joe Acton. As a courtesy to local champions, he would also drop a fall in two-out-of-three fall bouts instead of beating them in two straight falls. If you showed Lewis respect, he would not injure his opponent.

Born on a farm in Wisconsin before his wrestling career, he returned to a Wisconsin farm after retiring in 1899. After 17 years in the public spotlight, Lewis virtually disappeared from the public eye for the next twenty years. In this book, you will rediscover one of the greatest and most feared wrestlers of the 19th Century, Evan "The Strangler" Lewis.

Figure 1- The Strangler's Hold from February 2, 1890 edition of the Pittsburgh Gazette

Chapter 1 – "The Strangler" Arrives on the Scene

Evan "Strangler" Lewis was born in Ridgeway, Wisconsin on May 24, 1860. Lewis' father employed his time as a farmer and butcher. The young "Strangler" worked on the farm and developed his great strength from old fashioned farm work.

By the time Lewis was 22 years old, he stood 5'09" and weighed 175 pounds. Lewis travelled to Montana in May 1882, where he won a 64 man wrestling tournament.[i] After this victory, Lewis returned to Wisconsin to challenge Wisconsin Champion Ben Knight.

On March 21, 1883, Lewis defeated Knight for the Wisconsin Wrestling Championship. In 1885, Lewis moved to Madison, Wisconsin. He moved to improve his wrestling camp. During 1885, Lewis also defeated French champion Andre Christol and British Champion Tom Cannon.[ii]

In early 1886, Lewis took part in one of the most famous series of matches in his career. Lewis met Japanese wrestler Sorakichi Matsada in January 1886. Sorakichi stood 5'06" and weighed about 160 pounds. Lewis had a size and strength advantage although his strength advantage was slight.

In the first match, Lewis secured the stranglehold on Sorakichi, who fell to the mat with Lewis holding his neck. Carotid artery chokes are normally fairly safe unless you hold it on too long or you impinge the windpipe.

Lewis could do both because "The Stranglehold" was a guillotine choke not a rear naked choke as was previously believed. You can impinge the windpipe with the rear naked choke but it is harder to pull off. You can both choke and put pressure on the neck with the guillotine or as "The Strangler" called it, the stranglehold.

The referee did not react to the stranglehold quickly after Sorakichi Matsada passed out. By the time Lewis released the hold, Sorakichi's complexion was pallid. He could barely get to his feet.

Sorakichi Matsada was angry about the outcome and dared Lewis to match with him again but bar the stranglehold. Sorakichi's manner angered Lewis, who agreed to the terms. Lewis had a different plan for Sorakichi Matsada in the second match.

On February 15, 1886, Lewis met Sorakichi in Chicago, Illinois again. Sorakichi rushed Lewis in a match which lasted only a minute or so. When Sorakichi was unable to take Lewis down, he dropped to the floor in an attempt to roll to a hold. Lewis realized what Sorakichi was doing and grabbed a leg lock.

Leg locks are some of the most dangerous holds in grappling because by the time you feel pain and begin to tap, the damage has already been done to the limb. It does not appear Lewis intended to let Sorakichi tap. He put Sorakichi in a version of a knee bar with the intent of breaking his leg. Lewis only stopped due to catcalls from the fans.

Initially, Lewis was smiling after releasing the hold but his expression changed due to the reaction of the fans. Sorakichi had to be helped out of the ring. A medical examination showed that the limb was not broken but the ligaments were strained and damaged. Lewis offered no apology for what he had done.[iii]

The match with Sorakichi Matsada greatly increased his reputation as a "hooker", a wrestler skilled in submission wrestling. It also increased the fear both wrestlers and authorities experienced in dealing with Evan Lewis. Normally a mild mannered man outside the ring, he could be a brutal thug inside of it.

Lewis never escaped the taint of these early matches with Sorakichi Matsada. For the remainder of his career, Lewis' matches would be accompanied by charges of barbarism, brutality and cruelty. The picture of Lewis as a savage villain was established in the minds of both the wrestling press and wrestling public.

Lewis series with Sorakichi might have discouraged challengers for a while. However, on August 26, 1886, former foe Tom Cannon accepted Lewis' challenge. Lewis had challenged every wrestler for several months with little interest from anyone.

The match took place in Cincinnati, Ohio. The newspaper pundits claimed it was the most exciting match ever seen in the city. Unlike previous opponents, Tom Cannon initially succeeded in fending off the stranglehold. Cannon even surprised Lewis with a flying fall at 4 and a half minutes.

In the second fall, Lewis pressed the action for 9 minutes before he secured his stranglehold on Cannon.

Lewis squeezed the hold for 30 seconds before another slow referee broke the hold and declared the second fall for Lewis.

A grappler can induce unconsciousness on an opponent in as little as six seconds. A 30 second squeeze is a long time. Cannon clearly suffered the effects. It took him several minutes to get back to his feet. Despite the ten minute rest, Cannon could not continue the match.[iv]

Lewis' manager Parson Davies made a speech about Lewis always answering the bell and never forfeiting a match. When Cannon's friend Jimmy Faulkner challenged Lewis if he would forgo the stranglehold, Davies told the crowd Lewis did not wrestle for free. If Faulkner wanted to raise a side amount, they would consider his challenge. Lewis walked away with $200 side purse.

Davies' speech did not help build sympathy for his wrestler but Davies may not have been interested in improving his image. Being the villain could lead to lucrative promotion. Fans often pay for a match hoping to see the villain get his comeuppance.

Evan "Strangler" Lewis ended 1886 without a blemish on his record yet. His matches with Sorakichi Matsada and Tom Cannon enhanced his fearsome reputation. The 26 year-old Lewis finished his fourth year as a pro ready for some of the most prominent battles of his career.

Figure 2- Young Evan Lewis

Chapter 2 – Acton, Marriage and More Controversy

By the end of 1887, Evan Lewis would marry and continued to build his reputation as a wrestler to fear. First, Lewis would suffer his first defeat in the ring.

"Little Demon" Joe Acton, a British Champion, possessed a small but mighty frame. Acton stood 5'06" tall and weighed 155 pounds. Acton was even smaller than Sorakichi Matsada. However, even the mighty Clarence Whistler found himself unable to beat Acton.

Lewis met Acton in Chicago on February 8, 1887. Chicago was often the site of Lewis' greatest victories but on this night, Lewis could not hang with Acton. The match was for $500 a side.

The first fall in the catch-as-catch can bout ended with victory by Acton's half nelson. Acton hooked Lewis with the control hold and slowly wrenched Lewis onto his back for the first fall.

Lewis attacked in the second fall but could not secure his stranglehold. Instead Lewis entangled his leg with Acton and threw him to the ground. Acton's shoulders struck with a thud for the second fall in the match.

Lewis clearly fatigued in the second fall. Acton went back on the offensive and pinned Lewis again with a half nelson. Lewis ended the fall huffing and puffing.

Lewis growing desperate grabbed Acton, flung him over his head and slammed Acton to the ground with Lewis on top of him. The throw brought a grasp from the crowd. Acton was not injured though and secured another half nelson.

Lewis tried to resist but Acton turned him onto his back. Acton defeated Lewis three falls to one in the best three-out-of-five falls match. Acton walked off with the $500, while Lewis dealt with his first loss.[v]

Interestingly, Acton and Lewis would take part in a fixed match later. The fixed match enraged the fans so much both men matched up for a legitimate match a month later.

Before the second match with Acton in Chicago, Illinois, Lewis wrestled Jack Carkeek in Minneapolis. Lewis secured the stranglehold on Carkeek to end the first fall and the bout. Carkeek could not continue the match due to the effects of the stranglehold.

The April 12, 1887 edition of the *St. Paul Daily Globe* carried a story about the bout between two of the most feared professional wrestlers, Evan "Strangler" Lewis and "Little Demon" Joe Acton. The bout should have been a classic but the newspaper revealed a not-so shocking revelation. The match was a "hippodrome", a faked match. Suspicions of faked matches are found in newspaper accounts throughout Gilded Age combat sports history.

Why Lewis and Acton would take part in a faked match is not known but it may have been to stimulate betting on the match. Acton won the first fall. A man in the crowd was trying to get people at ringside to bet $100 to $60 that Lewis would win.

After Acton "won" the first fall in under ten minutes, this man and several backers again attempted to get wagers of $100 to $50 on Lewis' victory. Still no takers. If betting was the reason for the fix, the backers were unsuccessful in "conning the mugs".

Lewis won the next three falls with comparative ease. Considering Acton gave

Clarence Whistler all he could handle, it does not seem possible that even the talented Lewis could have beaten Acton so easily.

Prior to the 1915 New York Wrestling Tournament, which turned the tide of professional wrestling towards spectacle, many matches were legitimate. However, allegations of fixed matches arose in wrestling as early at the middle of the Nineteenth Century.

For the wrestlers, they may have fixed matches for a number of reasons. To stimulate interest in a legitimate championship match, to protect against injury or because the match would not afford them any real advantage.

Just like prizefighting, organized crime bosses might have had their hands into the wrestling scene also. Even William Muldoon was accused of fixing matches. It appears Muldoon did take part in some prearranged contests.

The only champion not known to have taken part in fixed matches was George Hackenschmidt, the World Wrestling Champion from 1901 to 1908.

Lewis not using the stranglehold also argues for a fixed match. Lewis frequently used this hold to win his matches and became enraged when officials tried to ban his pet hold.

In June 1887, Lewis and his manager Charles E. "Parson" Davies travelled to Pittsburgh to take on local champion

Thomas Conners. The match was purportedly for $1,000 a side.[vi]

On Saturday, August 5, 1887, Lewis travelled to Eau Claire, Wisconsin to wrestle Greco-Roman Champion Charles Moth. The match was conducted by catch-as-catch can rules in a two-out-of-three falls match. Lewis showed his superiority in an easy victory over Moth.

Lewis defeated Moth by pin fall within two minutes. Moth won the second fall by pin after ten minutes. Lewis completed the victory with another two minute pin fall.

The writer for the *St. Paul Daily Globe* reported Lewis appeared to exert little effort in the second fall. After rolling on the floor for a period, Lewis rolled to his back for the pin. The writer stated Lewis lost the second fall as "a courtesy".[vii]

The match with Moth showed another side of Lewis' character. If you angered Lewis, it would be very painful for you. If you paid him the proper respect, Lewis would not embarrass you even when you were not in his league. Lewis could have beaten Moth two straight falls but wanted to preserve Moth's reputation. Few men could get even one fall from "The Strangler".

J.P. Murphy's experience was quite different in October 1887. On October 29, 1887, Lewis wrestled Murphy in a three out of five falls match for $250 a side and 75 percent of gate receipts.

Whether it was the money or Murphy's manner, Evan Lewis wasted little time on Murphy.[viii]

Lewis beat Murphy in seven minutes for the first fall. Murphy vomited after the first bout. He surrendered the next two falls in 1 minute, 15 seconds and 5 minutes, 15 seconds respectively. Murphy hightailed it after the match.

The writer did not specify how Lewis won the first fall. Based on Murphy's actions after the first fall, he was the victim of a rough application of the stranglehold.

Interestingly, J.P. Murphy turned out to be John McPherson, an all-around athlete. Lewis and his manager conspired with McPherson and another athlete to try to pull a betting scheme on some other Madison, Wisconsin men.[ix]

McPherson and another athlete were supposedly going to compete in some field events. McPherson would pretend to have rudimentary knowledge of the events losing the first two tests to the other athlete. McPherson would then suddenly best his previous two efforts for the win.

The scheme was unsuccessful in conning the public. It also resulted in some heat on Lewis, who had been Madison's favorite son. While some of the press coverage of Lewis was unfair, he was often responsible for his bad reputation.

Evan Lewis ended 1887 by marrying Miss Hattie Thomas of Mineral Point, Wisconsin on Christmas Eve 1887.[x] "The Strangler" was on top of the world but storm clouds were forming on the horizon.

Figure 3 - Photo of Evan "The Strangler" Lewis

Chapter 3 – Victories in the Ring and Challenges Outside It

Evan Lewis started 1888 in a match with World Greco-Roman World Wrestling Champion William Muldoon. Muldoon agreed to throw Lewis in 15 minutes or be considered the loser. Throwing Lewis in 15 minutes was a tall order for any man even a powerful wrestler like Muldoon.

The February 4, 1888 edition of the *New York Sun* carried an account of the bout. Muldoon had been primarily touring with minstrel shows over the last two years. His reduced wrestling schedule showed on his physique which carried a little too much flesh. Muldoon usually weighed 220 pounds but may have been over 230 for this bout.

Lewis was light at 170 pounds after dealing with a serious illness in January 1888. Lewis did not tour after his marriage in Wisconsin. The cold Wisconsin weather may have adversely affected Lewis' health.

"Parson" Davies set the strategy for this match conducted under Greco-Roman wrestling rules. Greco-Roman wrestling banned holds below the waist. Only throws accomplished by the upper body were allowed. Davies told Lewis. "Don't worry about throwing him. Just don't let him throw you."[xi]

Lewis didn't try to throw Muldoon but couldn't resist trying to lock on the stranglehold. The match did not get started until 11 p.m. because both camps were arguing over the referee. They finally settled on Frank Glover.

The match conducted at the Casino Theater in Chicago, Illinois would be talked about for several weeks after the match. Lewis established himself as a major contender to the world title after this match.

Muldoon struck first by securing a back body hold and driving Lewis face first to the carpeted floor. Muldoon threw him with such force Lewis' face bounced off the floor.

Undeterred Lewis grabbed Muldoon in a neck hold and pulled him in front of him. Muldoon turned to land on his hands and knees. Lewis dove for a stranglehold but the more powerful Muldoon shrugged him off.

Over the next ten minutes, Lewis primarily played defense and only attacked when he saw an opportunity for the stranglehold. Muldoon could never secure a hold long enough to throw Lewis for the fall.

Muldoon's additional weight clearly affected him as he was exhausted after 10 minutes. Lewis, only interested in achieving the stranglehold which was shoved off each time, survived the effects of his illness better due to his tactics.

Muldoon really started to press Lewis in the last two minutes but could not secure a body hold. Muldoon walked to the front of the stage at the end of the fifteen minutes. "That's the best man I've met and I've met them all. I can't throw him in fifteen minutes."[xii] Glover declared Lewis the winner.

On his way back to the dressing room, the ungracious Lewis quipped, "He can't throw me at all, and I'm just about certain that I can throw him."[xiii] Lewis suffered a black eye from the early face plant to the carpet.

The champion Muldoon was in far worse shape. Both his eyes were blacked and he was bleeding from the mouth. Muldoon knew he would have to be in peak condition the next time he tangled with "The Strangler".

After the match, Muldoon and Lewis went on their own tour. Organized by "Parson" Davies, Muldoon and Lewis would meet any man including other wrestlers in a 15 minute match. If the wrestler could last 15 minutes in a Greco-Roman match with Muldoon or catch-as-catch can with Lewis, Davies would give them $50.[xiv]

It was arrangements like these so close to competitive or supposedly competitive matches, which caused members of both the press and the public to doubt wrestling match outcomes. After beating each other up two days before, Lewis and Muldoon are now partners in a tour.

The tour only lasted a few weeks before Lewis returned to answering challenges. On March 21, 1888, "The Strangler" travelled to Buffalo, New York to meet the challenge of Dennis Gallagher. The result of the match proved Evan Lewis' reputation for viciousness was well earned.

The headline in the March 22, 1888 edition of the *New York Sun* said it all: "The Strangler at his Old Game". The *Sun* called the match one of the most vicious contests in memory. The end of the match proved Lewis' inability to control his temper.

Lewis and Gallagher met in $250 prize match with Lewis agreeing to throw Gallagher five times in an hour. Gallagher felt so confident Lewis could not pin him five times he did not ask for Lewis' stranglehold to be banned.

Lewis attacked from the opening bell with the stranglehold. Gallagher expecting this tactic. He repeatedly fended off Lewis' attempts. Lewis secured the first fall in three minutes.

Frustrated, Lewis started throwing Gallagher around. Lewis even threw him into the laps of some mat side reporters. At the ten minute mark, Lewis faked a stranglehold transitioning to a leg grapevine and throw on Gallagher for the second fall.

Buffalo Mayor Becker was concerned about the roughness of the match. He refused to let the match continue if the stranglehold was not banned. Referee

James Wilson informed Lewis he could not use the stranglehold.

If Lewis was frustrated with Gallagher, he was flat angry now. Lewis grabbed Gallagher and slammed him to the mat. Gallagher successfully resisted having both shoulders pinned to the mat, when Lewis put the point of his elbow in Gallagher's throat.

Lewis began to compress Gallagher's windpipe. When Mayor Becker realized what was happening, he signaled to Police Superintendent Morris. Morris brought the match to an end.

Several big policeman entered the ring but they could not get Lewis to release his grip on the gurgling Gallagher. Finally, one of the policeman swung his club at Lewis. The blow missed but Lewis got the point. He released Gallagher.

Amid confusion in the ring and anger from the crowd, referee Wilson declared the match a draw.[xv] Lewis left Buffalo before city authorities decided to arrest him for almost starting a riot.

When Lewis signed to wrestled Englishman Jack Wannock, the Cornish Wrestling Champion, Chicago Mayor Roche would only allow the contest if the stranglehold was banned.[xvi] The match billed for the "World Title" took place on May 7, 1888 at Battery D in Chicago, Illinois. Wannock looked fit at 190 pounds but his face was flushed and nervous. Later, witnesses told the newspaper men Wannock had been in a tavern prior to the match. Lewis worried him so much Wannock needed liquid courage prior to the match.

Lewis proved Wannock's fears were justified. The match was a three-out-of-five falls match but Lewis decided to make it a short night.

In the first fall, both men approached each other warily until Lewis caught a leg grapevine. Lewis scrambled to a cross-buttocks lift and planted Wannock solidly on his back for the first fall at 6 minutes and 20 seconds.

Wannock did his best work in the second fall but it wasn't enough. Lewis started the fall with a headlock but Wannock secured a grapevine and threw

Lewis to his side. Lewis scrambled back to his feet.

Lewis secured a grapevine, which Wannock turned into a hip lock and lift. Lewis barely escaped and grabbed another grapevine. Wannock again almost pinned him with the hip lock lift.

A frustrated Lewis grabbed Wannock in a hammerlock. Lewis changed the hammerlock into a half-nelson and turned Wannock to his back. Lewis won the second fall in an identical 6 minutes and 20 seconds.

Wannock was bleeding from the mouth and tired to start the third fall. Desperate, Wannock charged Lewis, who deftly side-stepped the charging Wannock. Lewis applied a grapevine to a shoulder lock and planted Wannock on his back one more time.

Lewis vaulted over the top ropes to leave the ring, while Wannock staggered from the ring with help from his seconds. Alcohol did not help Wannock but a bout with "The Strangler" caused the most "drunkenness".

Even though the match was billed for the "World Championship", none of the authorities or press recognized Lewis as the World Champion. He was the most feared wrestler in the United States.

The following night in Chicago, Illinois, Lewis defeated Sorakichi Matsada in 13 minutes. Reporters generally credited Sorakichi with being a tougher opponent than Wannock.[xvii]

Lewis received an unpleasant surprise on July 3, 1888. Milwaukee Police arrested him on a charge of illegitimate parentage. Miss Annie Smith, the teacher at Lewis' hometown Barnevelt School, accused Lewis of both breach of promise and fathering her child out of wedlock.[xviii]

Lewis' marriage in December set off a chain of events which haunted him for some time. Lewis would find out how vicious a woman scorned could be. For the time being, Lewis had to surrender $300 or stay in jail.

On July 16th, Lewis answered the charges in a Milwaukee court room. Miss Smith sued Lewis for breach of promise.

She was asking for a judgment of $25,000.[xix]

Lewis would eventually settle the court case but not before it robbed him of most of the rest of the 1888 wrestling season. The suit also damaged his already controversial reputation with the wrestling public.

Lewis wrestled one last match to bring 1888 to a close. On December 19, 1888, Lewis defeated George Theodore, a Greek wrestler in front of a crowd of 400 people.

Lewis won the first fall in a minute. After a brief rest, Lewis won the second fall in 30 seconds. Apparently not wanting to lose the third fall in 15 seconds, Theodore claimed to be ill and forfeited the last fall and match to Lewis.ˣˣ

Lewis completed the 1888 campaign with a successful campaigns. His toughest match proved to be outside the ring though.

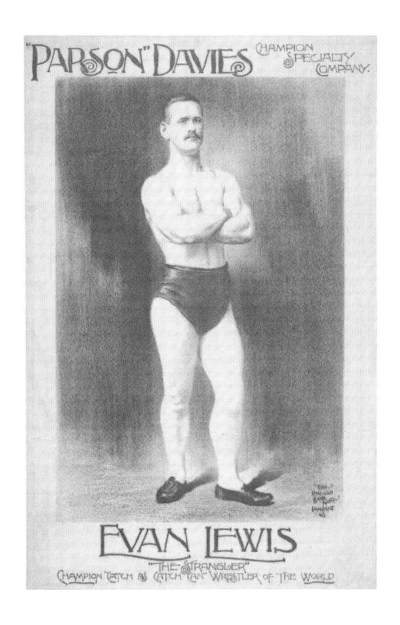

Figure 4 - Parson Davies' Promoting The Strangler

Chapter 4 – A Tough New Opponent

Lewis started out 1889 like most other years. He was relatively inactive during the winter months possibly because of travel difficulty from Wisconsin during this time of year.

Eventually, "The Strangler" emerged from his winter hibernation and began his 1889 campaign. His first victim would be capable French wrestler, Lucien March Christol. Christol previously wrestled World Champion William Muldoon in a losing effort.

Lewis and Christol met at the Olympic Theater in St. Paul, Minnesota. The match was for $200 a side. The difference in the physical condition of both men was pronounced. The muscular Lewis looked in peak condition around 180 pounds. Christol was smaller and pudgier.

Lewis took advantage of the size difference and pinned Christol for the first fall in one minute and twenty seconds. Christol made his best showing in the second round, where he bridged out of several pins before being pinned at the five minute mark.

In the third round, Lewis locked on the stranglehold. Christol submitted at the one minute mark. He also sported a noticeable ring around his neck for the remainder of the match.

Lewis finished the job by pinning him at the 2 and half minute mark and 2 minute mark respectively to complete the five falls in under one hour requirement.[xxi]

Despite being manhandled so thoroughly, Christol asked for a rematch in Minneapolis for a $200 purse. Christol wanted Lewis to agree to five falls in 30 minutes.

Ostensibly, Christol thought he could find a time limit short enough to keep from being pinned five times by Lewis. He was wrong. Two days later, Lewis threw Christol five times in under twenty minutes.[xxii]

"The Strangler" received a shock on April 20, 1889 in St. Paul, Minnesota. Unheralded wrestler D.A. McMillen beat Lewis for the first fall. Shocked, Lewis pinned McMillen three straight falls to win the match. Lewis singled out McMillen as his toughest opponent in a long time.^{xxiii}

On July 21st, Evan Lewis took on English champion Charles Green. Lewis not only beat Green but beat him up. Lewis won the first match in two minutes. The second fall lasted an hour and 3 minutes. Lewis secured the stranglehold to claim the second fall.

Lewis must have been using the hold as a neck crank also because Green's neck was injured. He surrendered the third straight fall in three minutes. Unlike Christol, Green did not want a rematch with Lewis.^{xxiv}

On August 7, 1889, Lewis engaged in a rematch with D. A. McMillen at the Coliseum in Omaha, Nebraska. While neither wrestler was in perfect condition, the fans raved about the contest for weeks after the battle. The *Omaha Daily Bee* called it "One of the most interesting exhibitions ever seen in this city".[xxv]

Lewis' normal muscular frame was covered with a layer of flab. McMillen possessed a more impressive physique but was covered with abrasions from his battle with a wrestler named Shellenbarger in Milwaukee, Wisconsin. The match reportedly lasted 14 hours.

After the sporting editor of the *Daily Bee* was selected as referee, the best three-out-of-five falls commenced. Lewis attacked almost immediately but the stronger McMillen prevented Lewis from grabbing a leg hold.

Eventually, Lewis secured the leg hold. He began to drag McMillen around the mat. McMillen was nearly standing on his head, when he completed a back somersault. McMillen regained his feat.

Lewis regained the leg lock with his right arm, while grabbing a half-nelson with his left arm. He twisted McMillen into the air and fell on him as both men crashed to the mat. Lewis secured the first fall at 8 minutes, 35 seconds.

The men took a fifteen minutes rest before commencing the second fall. McMillen started the fall determined to even the result. McMillen held the rare advantage of strength over Lewis. Outside of William Muldoon, Lewis held the strength advantage over all his previous opponents.

At the ten minute mark, McMillen secured a full nelson. Forcing Lewis' chin to his chest, spectators believed McMillen may break Lewis' neck.

Lewis forced himself to his feet one more time before collapsing on his back from the force of the full nelson. McMillen took the second fall at 14 minutes, 10 seconds.

As the third fall began, McMillen almost immediately secured a half nelson. Lewis was careful to stay close to the mat, so McMillen could not secure another full nelson.

McMillen ground on Lewis for the entire third fall. After 11 minutes, 5 seconds of hard struggle, Lewis succumbed to the McMillen for the second straight fall.

McMillen acquitted himself well but whether it was the 14 hour war, Lewis' grinding style or a combination of them both, McMillen fatigued badly.

Lewis resumed his previously successful tactic of securing the leg hold on his bigger opponent. Like he had in the past falls, McMillen exhibited surprising agility for such a big man. He repeatedly escaped Lewis' pin attempts through flips and head stands.

McMillen could not maintain his defense with his sapped energy levels. Lewis finally wrenched his shoulders down at 3 minutes, 10 seconds.

Lewis began the fifth and final fall in full out attack mode. McMillen resisted his efforts as best he could. Fans really enjoyed the energy level exhibited in the fall. After 16 minutes and 30 seconds, Lewis grabbed a leg lock and half-nelson for the final fall.

Despite the close call of losing two straight falls, "The Strangler" showed his resiliency in the fourth and fifth falls. The 1,200 spectators went home extremely happy.

Lewis did not try the stranglehold on McMillen. McMillen's strength might have led him to abandon his pet hold for this match. Lewis also respected McMillen, so he could have saved it for a last resort. It also may have been banned although none of the newspaper coverage of the event indicated a ban on the hold.

D.A. McMillen was not a huge star. McMillen's combination of skill and strength provided a tough challenge for Lewis. His challenge proved the old axiom "Styles make fights". While McMillen would not win a world title, his wrestling style proved more problematic for Lewis than more skilled champions.

Lewis ended the year wrestling old foe William Muldoon to several time limit draws. Lewis would have one more match with Muldoon before the latter retired to focus on his personal training business.

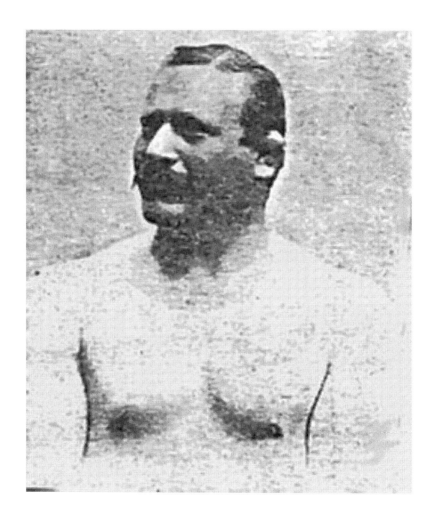

Figure 5 - Ernest Roeber, William Muldoon's Protégé

Chapter 5 – Old Foes and New Challenges

During January 1890, "The Strangler" came down with a strong case of Russian flu and pneumonia. Lewis was suffering from his various illnesses when he lost a one fall match to William Muldoon in 45 minutes.

He had to call off his second scheduled bout with Muldoon. For a while, it was feared he would not recover. Fortunately for both professional wrestling and "The Strangler", he did recover and made it hot for several wrestlers.

In June, he recovered sufficiently to wrestle Professor Frank Lewis of Minneapolis, Minnesota. Evan Lewis agreed to throw Professor Lewis in fifteen minutes or give him $25. Professor Lewis showed good defensive wrestling even throwing himself to the ground face first to prevent a pin fall. Lewis paid the Professor the twenty-five dollars.[xxvi]

Lewis continued his $25 tour by facing James Collins on June 25, 1890. This time, Lewis made sure to keep the $25 in his own pocket. After securing a body hold at two minutes, Lewis let Collins turn to his face several times before pinning him at 5 minutes, 20 seconds.[xxvii]

Lewis continued touring in the Midwest before embarking on a West Coast tour. Lewis' manager Parson Davies must have been getting Lewis back in shape during these tours. Lewis beat a number of local champions but did not challenge any top caliber opponents until August 1890.

On August 26, 1890, "The Strangler" met his first serious contender, David McLeod, in San Francisco. McLeod was champion of the local Olympic Club. Interest in the match generate a crowd of 2,500 spectators.

Lewis agreed to throw McLeod three times in an hour or be considered the loser. The match was contested for $400 a side. Lewis defeated the able McLeod but it was no easy match.[xxviii]

Lewis beat McLeod for the first fall in twenty-eight minutes. Lewis had an easier time in the second fall beating McLeod in eight minutes. Lewis took the third fall in thirteen minutes. In the third fall, McLeod actually scored three near falls on Lewis.

The 30 year-old Lewis would return to San Francisco for a bout with old foe Joe Acton. Lewis and "The Little Demon" contrived to wrestle fixed matches in the past. This bout appeared to be on the level.

The men battled in the new Wagwam for $500 a side. Lewis had to throw Acton twice in two hours or be considered the loser. The 186 pound Lewis threw the 162 pound Acton once but could not throw him a second time in the two hour time frame.[xxix]

Lewis returned home for Christmas as usual at the end of 1890. Both Lewis and his manager Parson Davies were attempting to secure a match for Lewis against Tom Connors.

Connors was reluctant to face Lewis, who was bigger and had the dreaded stranglehold. Connors continued to insist on stipulations Lewis would not agree to.

Lewis agreed to a match with William Muldoon but the forty year old Muldoon pulled out of the match. He informed "Parson" Davies he would not wrestle again. He did offer to match up his protégé Ernest Roeber with Lewis for $1,000 a side.

With Muldoon retired, Lewis, Tom Conners, Ernest Roeber and Jack Carkeek all claimed the title. Lewis wanted to secure the title in his own right.

In August 1891, old foe Sorakichi Matsada died probably as a result of his preference for the high life. Several newspapers carried stories of his death and incorrectly reported Lewis broke his ankle in their Chicago match.[xxx]

Evan Lewis would spend another year campaigning for recognition as the American Heavyweight Wrestling Champion. He would eventually gain the championship he coveted so badly.

Figure 6 - Ernest Roeber in front of his saloon in 1908. Roeber is on the left.

Chapter 6 – The Quest to Be Recognized as Champion

In Chicago, Illinois on March 21, 1892, "The Strangler" had to be satisfied in taking on Cornish Wrestling Champion John King. He really wanted to take on Ernest Roeber to secure his claim to American Heavyweight Wrestling Championship.

The match was contested in different styles in a three-out-of-five falls match. The first fall was contested by catch-as-catch can rules. Lewis won the fall in 9 minutes, 30 seconds.[xxxi]

The second fall was conducted in King's specialty, Cornish wrestling. King won this fall in 13 minutes. Lewis came back in the third fall conducted by side hold. Lewis won in 3 minutes, 10 seconds.

The fourth fall was conducted collar-and-elbow style. King's experience in this style helped him overcome Lewis in 15 minutes.

The match was decided by Greco-Roman rules in the fifth fall. Lewis took the fall and the match in five minutes. King was a formidable challenge but Lewis was returning to form.

Lewis finally secured a match with Muldoon's protégé Ernest Roeber for the opportunity to secure his claim on the American wrestling championship on March 2, 1893. To secure the match, he agreed to the stranglehold being banned for the match.

The match took place at the New Orleans Olympic Club, a venue with a capacity of 6,000 spectators. Promoters were unable to secure an anticipated pro boxing match between Tommy Ryan and his rival Dawson. The lack of a co-main event led to a disappointing gate of only 1,500 paying fans.[xxxii]

Lewis and Roeber came to the ring at 9 p.m. Lewis outweighed Roeber 185 to 178 pounds. Professor Duffy refereed the bout. Before starting the match, he announced the stranglehold was banned. Lewis wryly smiled while Roeber looked relieved.

The bout was contested in three-out-of-five falls. The first four falls would alternate between catch-as-catch can and Greco-Roman wrestling rules. The winner of the quickest fall would select the rules for the fifth fall if needed.

Immediately upon tying up, Lewis tripped Roeber to the floor and secured a half nelson. Roeber resisted as best he could but Lewis turned it into a half nelson and leg lock for the first fall at 7 minutes, 6 seconds.

Both wrestlers rested for ten minutes before contesting the second fall in Greco-Roman style. Roeber secured a double arm hold but Lewis dropped to the floor to avoid a flying fall. "The

Strangler" shrugged off Roeber's attempt to secure a half-nelson.

At the ten minute mark, Lewis and Roeber were so covered in sweat securing a hold was almost impossible. Both men took turns attacking each other. Roeber finally secured a half-nelson and turned Lewis over for a pinfall at 28 minutes, 12 seconds.

Lewis actually took the third fall in less than 30 seconds but Professor Duffy missed it. Lewis threw Roeber flat on his back with a neck hold and grapevine. He did it so quickly the referee missed what most of the other 1,500 spectators saw.

Lewis was enraged by both his loss in the second fall and the referee missing the fall to end the third. Lewis grabbed Roeber in a half-nelson and leg lock for his second pin fall in the third bout for the victory at 12 minutes, 9 seconds.

Lewis attacked Roeber for the fourth fall. Lewis initially took Roeber to the ground. After almost twenty minutes of ground grappling, Roeber wiggled out from underneath Lewis. Roeber secured a full nelson and turned Lewis onto his shoulders. Roeber won the fourth fall in 24 minutes, 43 seconds.

"The Strangler" secured the quickest fall in the match and by pre-match rules selected catch-as-catch can rules for the fifth fall. Lewis wasted no time in securing his victory. He threw Roeber heavily with a neck lock and hip hold in 1 minute, 3 seconds. The flying fall secured the American Heavyweight Wrestling Championship for Evan "The Strangler" Lewis.

A new challenger emerged for Lewis' belt almost immediately. Lewis defeated Martin "Farmer" Burns early in Burns' career. "The Farmer" had since developed a well-deserved reputation for being one of the most technical wrestlers of his era. Burns also packed surprising strength for a 165 pound man.

Lewis agreed to wrestle Burns for $1,000 a side. It must have taken Burns and his camp a while to raise the $1,000 because they did not reach an agreement until 1894.

Lewis spent most of 1893 touring around as the new American or "World" Wrestling Champion. Lewis and his camp often claimed the world title but it was a spurious claim at best.

Lewis did make time for one more match in 1893. After taking possibly staged bouts with Charles Moth and Jack King, Lewis wrestled a legitimate match with Duncan C. Ross in Chicago on November 20th. The championship did not mellow "The Strangler".

The account of the match did not state the stranglehold was banned but Lewis did not need his dread hold to hurt an opponent as he proved with Sorakichi Matsada.

Lewis had to win all three falls in the bout to win the $2,000 prize money and 80 percent of the gate receipts. Lewis intended to take the prize in this match.

Lewis threw Ross for the first fall in 13 minutes. The first fall was conducted by Greco-Roman rules. Greco-Roman wrestling rules were not considered an advantage for either man.

The second fall would be catch-as-catch can, Lewis' specialty. The third fall would be conducted in Ross' specialty, Cumberland wrestling rules.

Cumberland wrestling originated in Northern England. The wrestlers stand chest to chest with a secure back hold and head on each other's right shoulder.

The wrestling begins from this position. Ross did not get the chance to show his skill at this style of wrestling.

"The Strangler" secured a hammerlock and wrenched Ross over onto his back. Lewis used a slow pressure application of the hold to severely injure Ross' shoulder. Ross could not continue for the third fall.[xxxiii]

Lewis returned to Wisconsin for the holidays to prepare for the challenge of Martin "Farmer" Burns. A greater opponent was waiting for him though.

Figure 7 - Evan Lewis in his prime.

Chapter 7 – Illness and End of Title Run

Lewis caught typhoid pneumonia as 1894 began. It was the third time he caught the disease during his career.[xxxiv] He did recover in time to arrange a match with Martin "Farmer" Burns.

The title match was called off in April as Lewis was diagnosed with tuberculosis.[xxxv] Lewis was expected to die but made a full recovery from the flu or another case of pneumonia. The illness took him out of wrestling for most of 1894 though.

Lewis' frequent bouts of pneumonia and flu may have weakened his lungs. Lewis would contract lung cancer in 1917.

The disease would take his life two years later.

Lewis needed the rest of 1894 to recover from his illness. Martin "Farmer" Burns continued to wait for his opportunity, which finally came on April 20, 1895.

Martin "Farmer" Burns was a professional catch-as-catch can wrestler as well as wrestling and physical cultural trainer. He had success as a professional wrestler but is more famous as a trainer, primarily of the great Frank Gotch.

Martin "Farmer" Burns was born February 15, 1861 in Cedar County, Iowa. Both then and now, wrestling is in an Iowan's blood. Burns was already wrestling at an early age, when his father passed away. Like Lewis Burns began to do farm work to help support his mother and siblings, which allowed him to develop tremendous physical strength.

At 19, he was already winning professional wrestling matches. Burns worked to develop a huge neck rumored to be 20 inches in circumference. One of the feats he would perform later in life was to hang himself by the neck with a rope. Burns would walk away unscathed from his performance.

Burns started training other wrestlers in 1893. His most famous pupil would be Frank Gotch, who Burns defeated in 1899, when Gotch was 21. Burns would manage and train Gotch to the World Heavyweight Championship in 1908.

In 1914, Burns would publish an almost hundred page course on lessons in both physical culture and wrestling. Besides Gotch, Ed "Strangler" Lewis also followed Burns' training method.

Burns passed away on January 8, 1937 at 75 years of age in Council Bluffs, Iowa. Burns and his wife had three children, two sons and a daughter. Burns' wife passed away in 1930. After his daughter passed away in 1932, Burns' health began to deteriorate quickly.

In 1895, Burns was the number one contender for Lewis' title. The 34 year-old Burns challenged the 35 year-old champion in Lewis' favorite venue, Chicago, Illinois.[xxxvi]

Burns arrived in peak condition at 161 pounds. Lewis arrived woefully out of shape at 200 pounds. The Omaha Bee's reporter stated he was "fat as a prize pig".[xxxvii] It is arguable whether Lewis' illnesses accounted for his poor condition or whether the stress of nearly ten years near the top of the wrestling world finally took its toll.

Lewis still had something left in the tank despite his poor condition. Burns decided to play defensively in the first fall with the intent of letting Lewis burn some energy. Lewis obliged by doing most of the attacking.

Lewis secured a hammerlock but Burns shook it off. After a few more minutes of even wrestling, Lewis secured a half-nelson but again Burns shook it off. He wasn't three times lucky. Lewis secured another hammerlock.

This time Lewis turned Burns onto his back for the first fall. Unlike his match with Duncan Ross, Lewis was unable to injure Burns. Burns lost the fall but was still in peak condition.

Both men wrestled defensively in the second fall. It took a while for the action to get going. After a rather long stalemate, Lewis finally secured a hold on Burns leg but Burns shook him off.

Lewis secured a half-nelson but it proved to be his undoing in the second fall. Burns broke the half-nelson and achieved a quick turn. Burns motion threw Lewis over his head. Lewis crashed to the mat. The force of the slam dazed Lewis.

Burns moved in for the kill and threw him several more times. After Lewis crashed to the mat and stayed there, Burns turned Lewis onto his back with a hammer lock. Lewis fought viciously to escape the move but the rough handling by Burns made it impossible. Burns won the second fall at the 25 minute mark.

Even though Chicago was the site of many of Lewis' triumphs, spectators estimated 80 percent of the crowd favored "The Farmer". Burns made his camp in

Rock Island, Illinois across the state from Chicago along the Iowa border. Lewis also did little to endear himself to the public over the years.

The third fall started with Burns attacking Lewis but Lewis shrugging off all his hold attempts. Lewis secured both a double nelson and half-nelson but Burns escaped these holds.

Lewis violently rushed Burns, secured a body hold and landed a perfect flying fall. The fall was clean but the pro-Burns crowd booed the decision. Referee Charles Duplesis defended his decision to the crowd.[xxxviii] Lewis secured his last fall in the bout at 22 minutes, 8 seconds.

Burns decided he wasn't get paid by the hour in the fourth fall. He grabbed Lewis in a leg hold and half-nelson. With a twist of his body, he slammed "The Strangler" for a beautiful flying fall of his own. The time for the fourth fall was 1 minute.

Lewis decided it was time to pull out the dreaded stranglehold in a desperate bid to keep his championship. Lewis did not quite secure the lock around his neck. He contented himself with squeezing Burns' mouth and nose.

Burns escaped but Lewis secured a better hold and started to squeeze. Blood ran from Burns nose but he refused to submit. After about three minutes in the stranglehold, Burns broke loose.

Burns attacked like a wild man. Burns secured a body hold on Lewis and touched one shoulder to the floor but not both shoulders for the pin. Several times, Burns picked Lewis up off the floor with the intent of slamming him on his back but Lewis used the doubtful tactic of bracing on his head to prevent his shoulders and back being slammed to the ground.

Finally, Burns dropped Lewis onto his hands and knees but quickly secured the hammer lock. Despite Lewis struggling like a Wildman, "The Farmer" secured his shoulders to the mat for the fifth and deciding fall at 10 minutes, 10 seconds.

The 3,000 spectators cheered wildly for the new American Catch-as-Catch Can Wrestling Champion. Lewis returned to the dressing room, while the opportunistic "Parson" Davies challenged Burns for his other wrestler, Dan McLeod. It didn't appear an immediate rematch was in the cards for Evan Lewis.

Lewis made sporadic appearances on tours for the remainder of 1895. The relentless wrestling schedule and frequent illnesses were probably taking their toll on Lewis' aging body.

In January 1896, he made arrangements for wrestle J.C. Comstock. Whether the bout was on the level is another story. It was not widely reported on. Lewis won this battle in two straight falls.^{xxxix}

Lewis also failed to throw friend and fellow "Parson" Davies stablemate Dan McLeod. It is highly unlikely these matches were legitimate. Davies and Lewis were trying to build up McLeod's reputation for a challenge of Martin "Farmer" Burns.

Lewis also failed to throw Burt Scheller, the 170 pound wrestling champion in a Kalamzoo, Michigan match on February 11, 1896. This bout may or may not have been legitimate. It is possible the 36 year-old Lewis was unable to throw Scheller in fifteen minutes.^{xl}

By this time in his career, Lewis was preparing for retirement. The toll of being a hunted man both in and out of the ring plus his several bouts of pneumonia had taken their toll on his powerful body. While Lewis was still better than most, he knew he was no longer the wrestler every man including the world champion feared.

This point would be driven home on Lewis in the most humiliating defeat of his career in 1898. Lewis would take on a wrestler more powerful than Muldoon and as vicious as himself. "The Terrible Turk" would take a terrible toll on "The Strangler".

Figure 8 - Martin "Farmer" Burns Performing His Hanging Stunt

Chapter 8 – Defeat and Retirement

At the start of 1897, Evan Lewis broke with long time manager "Parson" Davies. The dissolution probably began when Davies challenged Burns for McLeod after Lewis' biggest defeat. A partnership of over 10 years ended over a tactless attempt to maintain a position of promotional power.

Lewis signaled this break by challenging the winner of the McLeod-Atherton match in January 1897. Both men declined to take on the aging but dangerous grappler.[xli]

Lewis also posted money with several sports offices trying to lure Burns back into a rematch for the American Catch-as-Catch Can Wrestling Championship. His efforts did not result in his desired rematch.

Lewis' only real contest was a match with "Gripman" John J. Rooney in Chicago, Illinois. Lewis threw Rooney seven times in an hour. Rooney only competed against Lewis because the stranglehold was banned.[xlii] In 1898, Lewis would find a foe eager to allow the stranglehold.

To kick off 1898, Lewis beat Jack King in a five style bout. Lewis won the warm-up bout three falls out of the first four.[xliii]

While Lewis was winning his tune-up bout, Yusuf Ismail, "The Terrible Turk", and old foe Ernest Roeber were preparing for a match in March 1898. The men agreed to meet in a Greco-Roman wrestling contest in New York City.

Yusuf Ismail was born in the Ottoman Empire on an unknown date around 1857. The giant Ismail stood 6'02" and weighed between 250 and 300 pounds. After a successful tour of Europe, he travelled to the United States in 1898.

Ismail chose his first match with Muldoon's protégé Roeber. Both men came to the ring in Madison Square Garden on the night of March 26, 1898 to meet in the highly hyped match. Roeber and Ismail entered the ring, a raised platform, in front of 6,000 paying spectators.

For this match, the ring was a padded carpet on a platform eight feet above the stage floor. The promoters made the ill-fated decision not to enclose the ring with ropes.

"The Terrible Turk" entered first wearing a turban and black overcoat. While Ismail was a ferocious competitor, he appeared unnerved by the hostile reaction of the New York fans.

Roeber entered the ring to cheers. He appeared to be in good condition but not good enough for what he was about to endure.

Referee Hugh Leonard started the match, which ended almost as quickly as it began. Ismail and Roeber circled each other warily for a minute and 30 seconds without achieving a hold. Suddenly as

Roeber skirted near the edge of the platform, Ismail charged him.

Roeber was knocked eight feet to the floor, where he landed on his side and back.[xliv] Roeber's seconds helped him to his feet as the crowd screamed foul. The fall caused a serious back injury, which would take almost a month to heal.

Ismail inexplicably started dancing in the middle of the ring after knocking Roeber off the platform. His celebration made it difficult for his handlers to argue Ismail knocked Roeber off the platform on accident.

Referee Leonard, who would be criticized for letting the men get too close to the edge, awarded the match to Ernest Roeber on a foul. The furious spectators left the venue disappointed and unlikely to pay for the pleasure of witnessing another wrestling match any time soon.

Despite the controversy over Yusuf Ismail's match with Ernest Roeber, 10,000 spectators paid to get into his match with Evan "The Strangler" Lewis in Chicago on June 20, 1898.[xlv] Fans got another controversial outcome.

Lewis and Ismail began the match. In less than three minutes, the much bigger Ismail secured "The Strangler's" own stranglehold. While Lewis struggled with being choked by the powerful Turk, referee Tim Hogan awarded the actual match to Lewis on a foul.

The fans screamed foul on their own. Even Lewis' backer, George Considine, made concessions the match may go on. However, referee Hogan refused to allow the match to continue. Chicago Police entered the ring and physically removed Hogan from the building.[xlvi]

After both camps agreed Lewis would receive the winner's purse of $2,225 dollars, the men restarted an exhibition match. They also agreed on C.O. Duplessis as the referee.

The exhibition bout would be best two-out-of-three falls. Oddly, Ismail did not learn much from the first match. He applied the stranglehold, which was now legal, in the first fall.

Duplessis was going to award the first fall to Ismail, when "The Terrible Turk" refused to release the hold after Lewis submission. Duplessis disqualified him giving the first fall to Lewis.

During the second fall, Ismail secured the stranglehold again. Lewis submitted at six minutes, 15 seconds. Ismail released the hold immediately this time.

After another 15 minutes rest, the men locked up again. Lewis was more successful at first. He shook off several of Ismail's holds. Finally, "The Terrible Turk" again grabbed a stranglehold. Lewis was forced to tap out again in 7 minutes, 10 seconds.

Lewis admitted, "I was licked; the Turk was the better man."[xlvii] Losing with his pet hold must have been humiliating. Ismail certainly did not take it easy on Lewis.

Ismail's fame was short lived. While returning to Europe aboard the *SS La Burgogne* on July 4, 1898, Yusuf Ismail was one of 600 passengers who drowned at sea.

Reportedly, Ismail carried a money belt of around 8 to 10 thousand dollars in coins around his waist. The weight of the belt pulled Ismail under water, where he drowned. A number of other Turkish wrestlers would take up "The Terrible Turk" nickname.

"The Terrible Turk" committed outrageous acts in pushing Roeber off a platform and getting disqualified twice against Lewis. Yet several newspapers made excuses for Ismail and his defeat of Lewis was celebrated.

On March 23, 1899, Evan Lewis wrestled his last recorded match against Burt Scheller in Kansas City, Missouri. The match would be contested in a best three-out-of-five falls fashion. To pull off the match, Lewis had to agree to the banning of the stranglehold.[xlviii]

Lewis was even heavier than usual at 208 pounds. Scheller weighed 187 pounds. The bout was for $250 a side. If part of the gate was also included, the gate would not be enough to pay any extra bonuses to participants.

Lewis made relatively short work of Scheller. Lewis took the first fall with a half-nelson and hammer lock in three minutes. He took the second fall with a hammer lock in six minutes, 45 seconds.

In the final fall, Lewis secured a full nelson for the final pin in three minutes, 15 seconds. The full nelson can be a very dangerous hold but Lewis did not use it to injure Scheller. Either he showed "The Strangler" the proper respect or Evan Lewis mellowed as he approached forty years old.

All great combat sports athletes have to call it quits one day. For Evan Lewis, 1899 was the year. Although promoters like "Parson" Davies would try to lure him back to the ring, "The Strangler" was done. The most feared wrestler of the 19th Century called it a career and retired for good.

Figure 9 - Yusuf Ismail, The Terrible Turk

Conclusion

Evan "Strangler" Lewis retired to his farm in Dodgeville, Wisconsin at the end of his wrestling career. One of the most famous wrestlers alive at the time, Lewis lived as a virtual recluse for the remainder of his life.

In 1902, "Parson" Davies attempted to get Lewis to tour with old foe Jack Carkeek. Lewis declined the invitation. Lewis was content to let his legend fade, while he returned to farming.

His legend did not completely fade though. When a young college wrestler from Wisconsin began his wrestling career, Robert Friedrich took the name of

Ed "Strangler" Lewis in homage to his home state hero.

Lewis' struggles with pneumonia were well documented. Whether pneumonia was a contributing factor or Lewis smoked tobacco, Lewis was diagnosed in 1917 with lung cancer.

The powerful Lewis would hang on for two years before finally succumbing to the disease on November 3, 1919. Lewis was 59 years old at the time of his death.

Evan Lewis is hard to categorize as a good guy or bad guy. His reputation was built on willfully maiming opponents in the ring. Lewis' ability with damaging submissions holds led him to be the most feared wrestler of his era.

His image was further injured when details of his love life were exposed before the public. Lewis was not unique among combat sports champions, when it came to his relationships with the opposite sex. Lewis' wrestling reputation made it easier for the public to dislike him though.

When Lewis retired, he did not chase the spotlight. He moved back to his beloved Wisconsin to live out the remainder of his days with his family. He refused several lucrative offers to trade in on his legend for some quick money.

Evan "The Strangler" Lewis was a complicated man and athlete. However, one thing was always clear. Don't make him mad in the ring. An angry "Strangler" could be extremely hazardous to your health.

Figure 10 - Evan "The Strangler" Lewis in the 1890s

Bibliography

Articles

Ehrman, Pete. *The Toughest Madisonian Who Ever Lived*. Madison Magazine, December 1991. WAWLI Redux No. 37 - http://www.wrestlingclassics.com/wawli/REDUXNos.31-40.html

Newspapers

Abbeville Messenger (Abbeville, South Carolina) April 6, 1886 edition

Bismark Daily Tribune (Bismark, Dakota Territory - Now North Dakota) April 26, 1889 edition

Daily Astorian (Astoria, Oregon) August 27, 1890 edition

Evening Bulletin (Maysville, Kentucky) May 10, 1888 edition

Great Falls Tribune (Great Falls, Montana) December 28, 1887 and December 26, 1888 edition

The Indianapolis Journal (Indianapolis, Indiana) March 3, 1893 edition

Jamestown Weekly Alert (Jamestown, Dakota Territory - Now North Dakota) July 19, 1888 edition

Kansas City Journal (Kansas City, Missouri) March 24, 1899 edition

Los Angeles Herald (Los Angeles, California) November 27, 1890 edition

New York Sun (New York, New York) August 27, 1886, March 22, 1888, March 27, 1898 and June 21, 1898 editions

News and Citizen (Morrisville, Vermont) March 11, 1886 edition

Omaha Daily Bee (Omaha, Nebraska) August 8, 1889 and April 21, 1895 editions

Pittsburgh Dispatch (Pittsburgh, Pennsylvania) February 2, 1890 and August 17, 1891 editions

Rock Island Daily Argus (Rock Island, Illinois) February 8, 1887 and January 30, 1897 editions

Salt Lake Evening Democrat (Salt Lake City, Utah) March 19, 1887 edition

Salt Lake Herald (Salt Lake City, Utah) August 18, 1891, February 14, 1894, April 23, 1894 and February 26, 1898 edition

San Francisco Call (San Francisco, California) January 19, 1896 edition

Sedalia Weekly Bazoo (Sedalia, Missouri) June 14, 1887 edition

St. Paul Daily Globe (St. Paul, Minnesota) April 12, 1887, August 7, 1887, October 30, 1887, November 1, 1887, May 8, 1888, July 5, 1888, April 13,

1889, April 17, 1889, July 22, 1889, June 24, 1890, June 26, 1890, March 22, 1892, February 12, 1896, March 14, 1897 and June 21, 1898 editions

Wheeling Intelligencer (Wheeling, West Virginia) November 21, 1893 edition

About the Author

Ken Zimmerman Jr. is married father of three, who lives in the St. Louis, MO Metro Area. Ken has a Bachelor of Science Degree from Washington University in St. Louis. Besides interests in genealogy and history, Ken is ranked in several martial arts.

If you like this book, you can sign up for Ken's newsletter to receive information about future book releases. You can sign up for the newsletter and receive bonus e-books by going to www.kenzimmermanjr.com and signing up for the newsletter.

Endnotes

Chapter 1

[i] Ehrman.

[ii] Ehrman

[iii] Abbeville Messenger (Abbeville, South Carolina) April 6, 1886 edition

[iv] The New York Sun August 27, 1886 edition. Lewis was preparing for a match with William Muldoon. This upcoming match may have led to the interest of Muldoon's hometown newspaper in an out-of-town match.

Chapter 2

[v] Rock Island Daily Argus (Rock Island, Illinois) February 8, 1887 edition

[vi] Sedalia Weekly Bazoo (Sedalia, MO) June 14, 1887 edition

[vii] St. Paul Daily Globe (St. Paul, Minnesota) August 7, 1887 edition

[viii] St. Paul Daily Globe, October 30, 1887 edition

[ix] St. Paul Daily Globe, November 1, 1887 edition

[x] Great Falls Tribune (Great Falls, Montana) December 28, 1887 edition

Chapter 3

[xi] New York Sun (New York, NY) February 4, 1888 edition

[xii] ibid

[xiii] ibid

[xiv] St. Paul Daily Globe, February 6, 1888 edition

[xv] New York Sun, March 22, 1888 edition

[xvi] St. Paul Daily Globe, May 8, 1888 edition

[xvii] Evening Bulletin (Maysville, Kentucky) May 10, 1888 edition

[xviii] St. Paul Daily Globe, July 5, 1888 edition

[xix] Jamestown Weekly Alert (Jamestown, Dakota Territory – Now North Dakota) July 18, 1888 edition

[xx] Great Falls Tribune (Great Falls, Montana) December 26, 1888 edition

Chapter 4

[xxi] St. Paul Daily Globe, April 13, 1889 edition

[xxii] St. Paul Daily Globe, April 17, 1889 edition

[xxiii] Bismark Weekly Tribune (Bismark, Dakota Territory) April 26, 1889 edition

[xxiv] St. Paul Daily Globe, July 22, 1889 edition

[xxv] Omaha Daily Bee (Omaha, Nebraska) August 8, 1889

Chapter 5

[xxvi][xxvi] St. Paul Daily Globe, June 24, 1890 edition

[xxvii] St. Paul Daily Globe, June 26, 1890 editions

[xxviii] The Daily Astorian (Astoria, Oregon) August 27, 1890 edition

[xxix] Los Angeles Herald (Los Angeles, California) November 27, 1890 edition

[xxx] Pittsburgh Dispatch (Pittsburgh, Pennsylvania) August 17, 1891 edition and Salt Lake City Herald (Salt Lake City, Utah) August 18, 1891 edition

Chapter 6

[xxxi] St. Paul Daily Globe, March 22, 1892 edition

[xxxii] The Indianapolis Journal (Indianapolis, Indiana) March 3, 1893 edition

[xxxiii] The Wheeling Intelligencer (Wheeling, West Virginia) November 21, 1893 edition

Chapter 7

[xxxiv] The Salt Lake Herald (Salt Lake City, Utah) February 14, 1894 editions

[xxxv] The Salt Lake Herald, April 23, 1894 editions

[xxxvi] Omaha Daily Bee (Omaha, Nebraska) April 21, 1895 edition

[xxxvii] Ibid

[xxxviii] Ibid

[xxxix] San Francisco Call (San Francisco, California) January 18, 1896 edition

[xl] St. Paul Daily Globe (St. Paul, Minnesota) February 12, 1896 edition

Chapter 8

[xli] Rock Island Argus (Rock Island, Illinois) January 30, 1897 edition

[xlii] St. Paul Daily Globe (St. Paul, Minnesota) March 14, 1897 edition

[xliii] Salt Lake Herald (Salt Lake City, Utah) February 26, 1898 edition

[xliv] New York Sun (New York City, New York) March 27, 1898 edition

[xlv] St. Paul Daily Globe, June 21, 1898 edition

[xlvi] New York Sun, June 21, 1898 edition

[xlvii] St. Paul Daily Globe, June 21, 1898 edition

[xlviii] Kansas City Journal (Kansas City, MO) March 24, 1899 edition

Made in the USA
Las Vegas, NV
02 March 2021